Jewelry on a String

Are you captivated by all those pretty little snippets of pre-strung beads, but not sure how to use them? This book has the answers, with gorgeous projects featuring before and after photos, step-by-step instructions, and basic jewelry-making tips.

LEISURE ARTS, INC. • Maumelle, Arkansas

Turquoise Necklace, Bracelet, & Earrings

SHOPPING LIST

- ☐ 30mm x 22mm turquoise pillow bead string for necklace and earrings
- ☐ 8mm silver bead string for necklace
- ☐ 4mm silver bead string for necklace
- ☐ silver toggle clasp for necklace
- ☐ silver decorative crystal head pins for necklace and earrings
- ☐ silver nylon-coated beading wire for necklace and bracelet
- ☐ medium and large silver jump rings for necklace and bracelet
- ☐ 10mm wood bead string for bracelet
- ☐ turquoise chip bead string for bracelet
- ☐ 4mm silver corrugated beads for bracelet
- ☐ clear seed beads for bracelet
- ☐ silver chain for bracelet
- ☐ silver butterfly charm for bracelet
- ☐ silver lobster clasp for bracelet
- ☐ 2 silver ear wires for earrings
- ☐ silver crimp beads and crimp tool for necklace and bracelet
- ☐ wire cutters, chain-nose pliers (2 pair), and round-nose pliers

Just a few chunky turquoise beads, paired with silver and wood beads, are all you need for an awesome jewelry combo!

To make the Necklace:

Approx. Length: 18"

1. Make a bead dangle (page 31) with a turquoise pillow bead and a crystal head pin. Make a total of 3 bead dangles.
2. Use a crimp bead (page 32) to attach a medium jump ring to a 27" wire length. Thread silver beads and turquoise bead dangles on the wire until the beaded section is about 16 1/2" long.
3. Use a crimp bead to attach a medium jump ring on the other end of the necklace.
4. Attach a toggle clasp piece to each jump ring (page 31).

To make the Bracelet:

1. Cut a piece of chain the desired bracelet length, minus the length of the closed clasp.

2. Use a crimp bead (page 32) to attach a 12" wire length to a medium jump ring *(Photo 1)*.

Photo 1

3. Thread turquoise chip beads and silver corrugated beads on the wire length until the beaded length is the same or just a bit longer than the chain cut in Step 1.

4. Repeat Steps 2-3 with the wood and clear seed beads.

5. Attach a large jump ring to one end of the chain, wood bead strand, and turquoise bead strand *(Photo 2)*. Repeat with the remaining chain and beaded strand ends.

Photo 2

6. Attach the clasp (page 31) to a large jump ring on one end of the bracelet. Attach the butterfly charm to the opposite jump ring.

To make each Earring:

1. Make a bead dangle (page 31) with a turquoise pillow bead and a crystal head pin.

2. Attach the bead dangle (page 31) to an ear wire.

Knotted Pearl Bracelet

SHOPPING LIST

- ☐ 2 strings of 3 coordinating colors pearl-finish glass beads (about 6mm x 8mm)
- ☐ 2 large silver cones
- ☐ 3-hole jeweled spacer bars (we used 4)
- ☐ silver toggle clasp
- ☐ white braiding cord
- ☐ jeweler's glue

To make the Bracelet:

1. Measure both cones and the closed clasp; add these together. Subtract this number from the desired finished bracelet length.

2. Cut 9 54" braiding cord lengths. Holding one end of each cord length, tie a loose overhand knot (page 32) about 3" from one end. Tape the knot down.

3. Divide the cords into 3 groups of 3. Tie 3 square knots (page 32) with each group of cords ***(Fig. 1)***.

Fig. 1

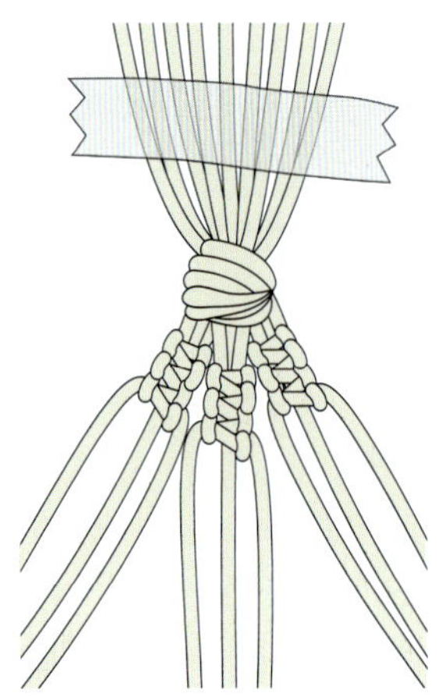

4. Thread a bead on the center cord of each group. Switch the cords as shown in **Fig. 2** and tie a square knot. Repeat twice, using a different color bead for each row.

Fig. 2

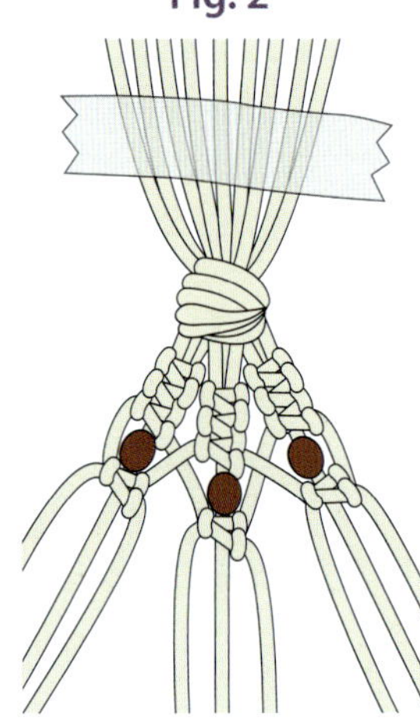

5. Thread a spacer bar on the cords.
6. Repeat Steps 4-5 until the bracelet is the measurement determined in Step 1.
7. Tie 3 square knots with the 3 groups of cords as you did in Step 1.
8. Slide a cone and a clasp end on the cords. Thread the cords back through the cone. Tie an overhand knot around all 9 cords as close as possible to the upper end of the cone. Apply glue to the knot. Once dry, trim the cord ends close to the knot.
9. Untie the overhand knot on the beginning end of the bracelet. Repeat Step 8 with the remaining cone and clasp end.

Easy square knots hold these neutral-toned beads in line, while creating a stunning cuff-style bracelet!

5-Strand Bracelet, Necklace, & Earrings

SHOPPING LIST

- ☐ 5 strings of coordinating beads (all about the same size; we used 6mm x 9mm oval coral beads and 6mm metal, bamboo, turquoise, and silver stardust beads)
- ☐ 4mm silver beads
- ☐ silver multi-strand clasp and spacer bar set for bracelet
- ☐ silver nylon-coated beading wire for bracelet
- ☐ silver crimp beads and crimp tool for bracelet
- ☐ silver chain for bracelet and necklace
- ☐ silver pre-made chain necklace
- ☐ silver eye pins for necklace
- ☐ silver head pins for necklace and earrings
- ☐ silver jump rings for necklace and earrings
- ☐ 2 silver ear wires for earrings
- ☐ wire cutters, chain-nose pliers (2 pair), and round-nose pliers

The bracelet is the star here. Five strings of beads come together in one fabulous bracelet. Use the remaining beads to make a necklace and earrings.

To make the Bracelet:

1. Cut ten 1 1/4" lengths of chain; set aside 5 lengths. Attach one chain length (page 31) to each loop on one clasp end. Use a crimp bead (page 32) to attach a 9" wire length to the last link of each chain. Thread a 4mm silver bead on each wire length. Thread the wire lengths through a spacer bar.

2. To determine the beaded strand lengths, measure the clasp and chains completed in Step 1; multiply by 2. Subtract this measurement from the desired finished length. The resulting measurement will be the length of the beaded strands. Thread the coordinating beads on each wire length. Thread the remaining spacer bar on the wire lengths. Add or remove beads until the spacer bar lies straight and even.

3. Thread a 4mm silver bead on the first wire length and use a crimp bead to attach a chain length cut in Step 1. Attach the the remaining clasp end to the opposite end of the chain. Repeat with the remaining wire lengths.

To make the Necklace:

1. Make 3 bead dangles (page 31) with 2 beads and a head pin and 3 long bead dangles with 3-5 beads and a head pin.

2. To make a beaded connector, thread 3 beads on an eye pin. Make a loop (page 31) at the wire end ***(Photo 1)***. Make 2 beaded connectors.

Photo 1

3. Attach a dangle (page 31) to a 1 3/8" chain length. Attach the remaining dangles to the connectors.

4. Attach jump rings to the chain with the dangle, connectors, and long dangles. Slide the pieces on the necklace.

To make each Earring:

1. Make 3 bead dangles (page 31) with 3-4 beads and a head pin.

2. Attach the dangles to a jump ring (page 31).

3. Attach the jump ring to an ear wire.

Burlap & Lace Necklace, Earrings, & Ring

SHOPPING LIST

- ☐ 8mm fresh water pearl bead string
- ☐ burlap-covered bead string for necklace and earrings
- ☐ white flower sliders string for necklace and ring
- ☐ 24" of 3/4" wide lace for necklace
- ☐ gold chain for necklace
- ☐ gold toggle clasp for necklace
- ☐ gold jump rings for necklace
- ☐ gold nylon-coated beading wire for necklace
- ☐ gold crimp beads and crimp tool for necklace
- ☐ stretch cord for necklace and ring
- ☐ jeweler's glue for necklace and ring
- ☐ gold head pins for earrings
- ☐ gold eye pins for earrings
- ☐ 2 gold ear wires for earrings
- ☐ wire cutters, chain-nose pliers (2 pair), and round-nose pliers

Create a fresh look when you combine the rustic texture of burlap-covered beads with white flower sliders and classic fresh water pearl beads.

To make the Necklace:

Approx. Length: 26"

1. Cut an 8" gold chain length. Use a jump ring (page 31) to attach one chain end to one end of the clasp.

2. Use a crimp bead (page 32) to attach a 24" wire length to the remaining chain end.

3. Fold one end of the lace onto itself about 3/4"; thread the lace on the wire attached to the chain. Thread a burlap bead on the wire. Pull the lace close around the bead and fold it again. Thread it on the wire *(Fig. 1)*. Ending with folded lace, continue adding burlap beads and folding lace until you've used 7 burlap beads. Trim the excess lace.

4. Thread the pearl beads on the wire until the pearl section is about 11" long. Use a crimp bead to attach the remaining clasp end.

Fig. 1

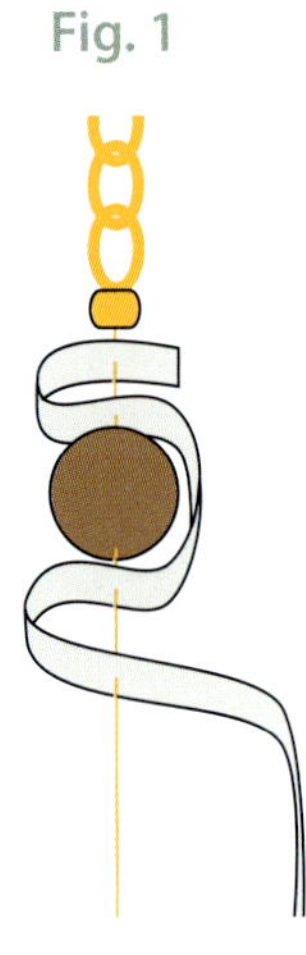

5. Use the stretch cord to securely tie 2 flower sliders to the chain. Apply a drop of glue to each knot. Once dry, trim the cord ends.

To make each Earring:

1. Make a bead dangle (page 31) with a pearl and a head pin.
2. To make a beaded connector, thread a pearl bead on an eye pin. Make a loop (page 31) at the wire end *(Photo 1)*. Make 2 pearl connectors and a burlap bead connector.

Photo 1

3. Attach the dangle and connectors (page 31) to an ear wire.

To make the Ring:

1. Cut two 12" stretch cord lengths. Thread a cord length through each set of loops on the back of a flower slider *(Photo 1)*.

Photo 1

2. Thread 10-12 pearl beads on each cord. Loosely tie the cord ends together and try the ring on for size. Add or remove beads as necessary. Tie all the cords together with a surgeon's knot *(Fig. 2)* and apply a drop of glue to the knot. Once dry, trim the cord ends.

Fig. 2

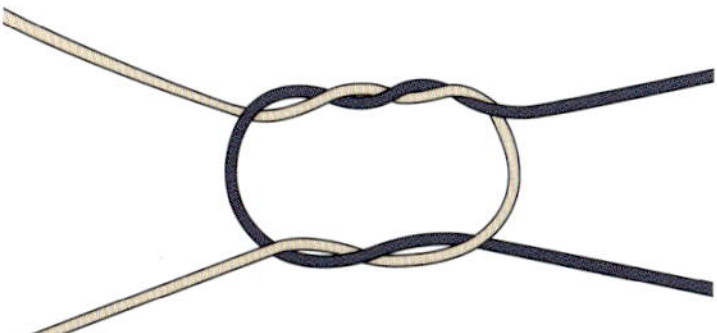

Classic Pearl Necklace & Earrings

SHOPPING LIST

- ☐ 6mm and 8mm pearl bead strings
- ☐ silver jeweled toggle clasp for necklace
- ☐ silver eye pin for necklace
- ☐ silver jump rings for necklace
- ☐ silver nylon-coated beading wire for necklace
- ☐ silver crimp beads and crimp tool for necklace
- ☐ silver decorative head pins for necklace and earrings
- ☐ 2 silver ornate connectors for earrings
- ☐ 2 silver ear wires for earrings
- ☐ wire cutters, chain-nose pliers (2 pair), and round-nose pliers

A classic strand of pearls with matching earrings never goes out of style. Modernize the look with 2 sizes of pearls and a jeweled clasp.

To make the Necklace:

Approx. Length: 23"

1. Use a crimp bead (page 32) to attach a jump ring to a 27" wire length. Thread 6mm pearls on the wire until the beaded section is about 20$^{1}/_{2}$" long. Use a crimp bead to attach the remaining wire end to a jump ring.

2. Use a crimp bead to attach a 29" wire length to the jump ring on the beaded strand. Thread 8mm pearls on the wire until the beaded section is about 21$^{1}/_{2}$" long. Use a crimp bead to attach the wire end to the remaining jump ring.

3. Attach the clasp to the jump rings (page 31).

4. To make the beaded connector, thread an 8mm pearl on the eye pin. Make a loop (page 31) at the wire end *(Photo 1)*.

Photo 1

5. Make a bead dangle (page 31) with a 6mm pearl and a head pin.

6. Attach the dangle (page 31) to the beaded connector and the beaded connector to the clasp.

To make each Earring:

1. Make a bead dangle (page 31) with an 8mm pearl and a head pin.

2. Attach the dangle to the ornate connector and the connector to the ear wire.

Purple Necklace, Bracelets, & Earrings

SHOPPING LIST

- ☐ 6 silver bead caps
- ☐ assorted purple seed bead string
- ☐ assorted purple bead string
- ☐ 6mm crystal bicone bead string
- ☐ 8mm purple crystal faceted round bead string for necklace and bracelet
- ☐ large-link silver chain for necklace
- ☐ purple braiding cord for necklace
- ☐ silver lobster clasp for necklace
- ☐ silver jump rings for necklace
- ☐ jeweler's glue for necklace
- ☐ decorative silver head pins for necklace and earrings
- ☐ assorted silver beads for necklace and bracelets
- ☐ silver tube beads for bracelets
- ☐ 2 jeweled spacers for bracelets
- ☐ 2 silver toggle clasps for bracelets
- ☐ silver nylon-coated beading wire for bracelets
- ☐ silver crimp beads and crimp tool for bracelets
- ☐ 2 silver ear wires for earrings
- ☐ wire cutters, chain-nose pliers (2 pair), and round-nose pliers

Start with a single strand of decandent purple beads, add a mixture of violet-hued seed beads and sparkly silver and crystal beads and you've got a jewelry set fit for a queen!

To make the Necklace:

Approx. Length: 26"

1. Cut a $25\frac{1}{2}$" chain length and a 1" chain length. Attach the lobster clasp (page 31) to one end of the long chain length. Attach a jump ring to the other end. Attach the short chain length to the center of the necklace.

2. Knotting the cord to the chain ends, weave the braiding cord through the necklace chain. Apply a drop of glue to each knot. Once dry, trim the cord ends.

3. Make a bead dangle (page 31) with 7 beads and a decorative head pin. Make another bead dangle with a very large bead, bead caps, and a decorative head pin. Use jump rings to attach the dangles to the short hanging chain on the necklace.

4. Fold a 12" braiding cord length in half and loop through the upper bead dangle jump ring *(Fig. 1)*. Thread beads on the cord ends. Knot the ends close to the beads and trim the excess cord. Apply a drop of glue to each knot.

Fig. 1

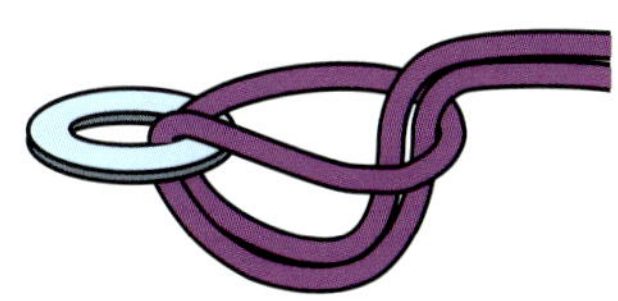

To make each Bracelet:

1. Use a crimp bead (page 32) to attach a 12" wire length to one toggle clasp end.

2. Thread beads (and spacers) on the wire. Check the bracelet size, adding or removing beads until the bracelet is the right length.

3. Use a crimp bead to attach the remaining clasp end to the bracelet.

To make each Earring:

1. Make a bead dangle (page 31) with beads, a bead cap, and decorative head pin.

2. Attach the dangle (page 31) to an ear wire.

Large-hole Bead Necklaces

SHOPPING LIST

- ☐ large-hole beads and spacer beads
- ☐ pendant (large or small)
- ☐ pre-made necklace **OR** leather cord, foldover cord ends, jump rings, desired clasp, jeweler's glue, and chain-nose pliers

To make the Necklace:

Approx. Length: varies

1. If using a pre-made necklace, slide the beads, spacers, and pendant on the necklace.

2. If making your own necklace, cut the desired length of leather cord. Slide the beads, spacers, and pendant on the cord. Lay one end of the cord in the foldover cord end, apply a drop of glue, and use the chain-nose pliers to fold the tabs down over the cord *(Fig. 1)*. Repeat for the opposite end of the cord. Use a jump ring (page 31) to attach the clasp to the cord end. Attach a jump ring to the remaining cord end.

Fig. 1

Large-hole beads and spacer beads are everywhere. Surrounding a pretty pendant on a pre-made necklace (or make your own), the beads create a bold statement for your wardrobe.

Contemporary Pearl Necklace & Bracelet

SHOPPING LIST

- ☐ 6mm fresh water pearl bead string
- ☐ 4mm silver corrugated beads
- ☐ silver head pins for necklace
- ☐ silver eye pins for necklace
- ☐ pre-made multi-cord choker necklace
- ☐ antique silver toggle clasp for bracelet
- ☐ silver nylon-coated beading wire for bracelet
- ☐ silver crimp beads and crimp tool for bracelet
- ☐ wire cutters, chain-nose pliers (2 pair), and round-nose pliers

To make the Necklace:

1. Make a bead dangle (page 31) with 1-3 beads and a head pin. Make 13 dangles.

2. To make a beaded connector, thread 3 beads on an eye pin. Make a loop at the wire end ***(Photo 1)***. Make 3 connectors.

Photo 1

3. Attach a dangle (page 31) to each connector. Slide the dangles and connectors on the choker.

Pearls take on a contemporary appeal when paired with black and silver. A multi-cord pre-made choker makes it easy to slide on pearl dangles. The antique silver toggle on the bracelet ties it all together.

To make the Bracelet:

1. Use a crimp bead (page 32) to attach a 12" wire length to one end of the clasp.
2. Alternating pearl and silver beads, thread the beads on the wire. Check the bracelet size, adding or removing beads until the bracelet is the right length.
3. Use a crimp bead to attach the remaining clasp end.

Gold Chain Bracelet

SHOPPING LIST

- ☐ mixed bead string
- ☐ 4mm gold corrugated beads and gold seed beads (to lengthen bracelet if necessary)
- ☐ gold chain
- ☐ gold toggle clasp
- ☐ gold nylon-coated beading wire
- ☐ gold jump rings
- ☐ gold crimp beads and crimp tool
- ☐ wire cutters and chain-nose pliers (2 pair)

To make the Bracelet:

1. Cut 2 pieces of chain the desired bracelet length, minus the length of the closed clasp.
2. Use a crimp bead (page 32) to attach a 12" wire length to one end of the clasp.
3. Thread the beads on the wire until the beaded length is the same or just a bit longer than the chains cut in Step 1.
4. Use a crimp bead to attach the remaining clasp end to the beaded length.
5. Use a jump ring (page 31) to attach the chain ends to the clasp ends

Sometimes the bead string that you've fallen in love with is not quite long enough to make a bracelet. Just add a few small beads in between the larger beads.

Interchangeable Pendant Necklace

SHOPPING LIST

- ☐ 6mm multi-colored faceted bead string
- ☐ silver diamond-shaped bead string
- ☐ 4mm green crystal bead string
- ☐ 4mm olive crystal bead string
- ☐ 6mm purple crystal bead string
- ☐ antique silver turtle pendant with an attached large jump ring
- ☐ silver lobster clasp
- ☐ silver jump ring
- ☐ silver nylon-coated beading wire
- ☐ silver crimp beads and crimp tool
- ☐ wire cutters
- ☐ large jump rings, large bail, or ribbon (optional, to attach the other pendants)

Use several strings of beads in coordinating colors and shapes to make a very basic necklace. It will become your "go to" accessory when you change out the pendants.

To make the Necklace:

Approx. Length: 25"

1. Use a crimp bead (page 32) to attach a 36" wire length to the clasp.
2. Thread the beads on the wire until the beaded section is about 24" long.
3. Use a crimp bead to attach a jump ring to the end of the beaded length.
4. Slide the pendant on the necklace.

* *To change the pendant, attach a large jump ring or large bail to the pendant and slide it on the necklace. Or, you can tie on a pendant with a coordinating ribbon.*

Velvet Necklace, Earrings, & Bracelet

SHOPPING LIST

- ☐ velvet ribbon pre-made necklace with attached large jump rings
- ☐ 2 bicone crystals, crystal round beads, and bead dangle clusters bead strings
- ☐ silver nylon-coated beading wire for necklace and bracelet
- ☐ silver crimp beads and crimp tool for necklace and bracelet
- ☐ silver lobster clasp and extension chain for bracelet
- ☐ silver jump rings for bracelet
- ☐ 4mm silver beads for bracelet and earrings
- ☐ 2 silver ear wires for earrings
- ☐ 2 silver head pins for earrings
- ☐ wire cutters, chain-nose pliers (2 pair), and round-nose pliers

An adjustable-length velvet necklace and bead dangle clusters join forces for a unique adornment. Make matching earrings and a bracelet to complete the look.

To make the Necklace:

Approx. Length: 25"

1. Use a crimp bead (page 32) to attach one jump ring on the ribbon necklace to a 9" wire length. Thread beads and bead dangle clusters on the wire.

2. Use a crimp bead to attach the beaded section to the remaining jump ring on the other end of the necklace.

To make the Bracelet:

1. Attach a jump ring (page 31) to the clasp. Use a crimp bead (page 32) to attach the clasp jump ring to a 12" wire length.

2. Thread silver beads, bicone beads, round beads, and bead dangle clusters on the wire. Check the bracelet size, adding or removing beads until the bracelet is the right length.

3. Use a crimp bead to attach the extension chain (add a jump ring if the chain doesn't have one).

To make each Earring:

1. Make a bead dangle (page 31) with 4 silver beads, a round bead, 2 bicone beads, and a head pin.

2. Attach the bead dangle (page 31) to an ear wire.

Pink Bow Pearl Necklace, Bracelets, & Earrings

SHOPPING LIST

- ☐ 8mm and 4mm pearl bead strings
- ☐ silver lobster clasp for necklace
- ☐ 2 silver 3-strand spacer ends for necklace
- ☐ silver crimp beads and crimp tool for necklace
- ☐ silver nylon-coated beading wire for necklace
- ☐ two 12" lengths of 5/8"w pink satin ribbon for necklace and bracelets
- ☐ stretch cord for bracelets
- ☐ jeweler's glue for bracelets
- ☐ flexible wire beading needle for bracelets (optional)
- ☐ silver decorative head pins for earrings
- ☐ 2 silver heart-shaped jump rings for earrings
- ☐ 2 silver ear wires for earrings
- ☐ wire cutters, chain-nose pliers (2 pair), and round-nose pliers

Pearls and pink ribbon combine for a sweetly feminine look. Top it off with earrings made with heart-shaped jump rings.

To make the Necklace:

Approx. Length: 26"

1. Use a crimp bead (page 32) to attach one clasp end to a 14" wire length. Thread 30 8mm pearls on the wire. Use a crimp bead to attach a spacer end to the strung pearls. Repeat with the remaining clasp end, wire, beads, and spacer end for the other side of the necklace.

2. Use a crimp bead to attach an 8" wire length to the innermost loop on a spacer end. Thread 16 8mm pearls on the wire. Use a crimp bead to attach the strung pearls to the corresponding loop on the remaining spacer end.

3. Repeat Step 2 with a 9" wire length and 18 8mm pearls on the middle loop and then again with a 10" wire length and 20 8mm pearls on the outermost loop.

4. Tie a ribbon bow around the necklace as shown in the photo.

To make the Bracelets:

1. With a bead stop at one end *(Fig. 1)*, thread about 48-50 4mm pearls on a 12" stretch cord length.

Fig. 1

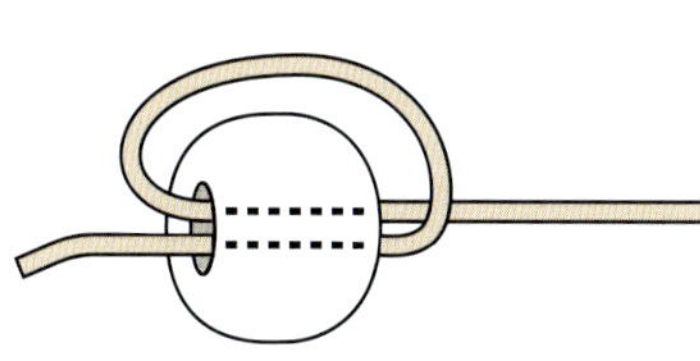

2. Check the bracelet size, adding or removing pearls until the bracelet is the right length. Remove the bead stop. Tie the cord with a surgeon's knot *(Fig. 2)* and apply a drop of glue to the knot. Once dry, trim the cord ends.

Fig. 2

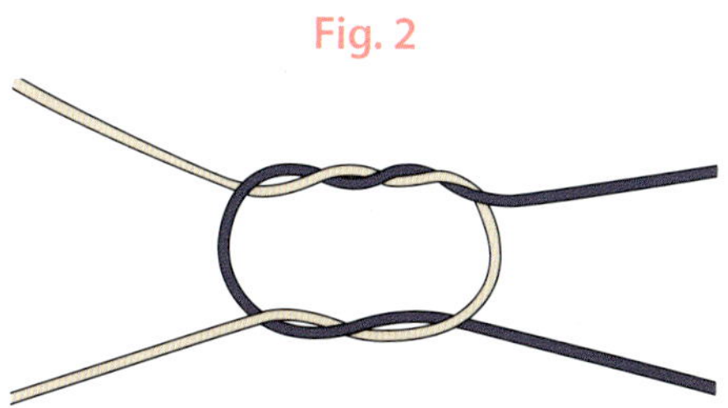

3. Repeat Steps 1-2 to make two more 4mm pearl bracelets.
4. Repeat Steps 1-2 with about 35 4mm pearls and 8 8mm pearls.
5. Tie the bracelets together with a ribbon bow.

To make each Earring:

1. Make a bead dangle (page 31) with an 8mm pearl and a head pin.
2. Use a heart-shaped jump ring to attach (page 31) the dangle to an ear wire.

Stretchy Bracelets

SHOPPING LIST

- ☐ desired bead or slider string (you'll need 2 or more strings of the sliders)
- ☐ clear seed beads (optional)
- ☐ assorted coordinating beads (optional)
- ☐ silver charm with attached jump ring (optional)
- ☐ ribbon (optional)
- ☐ stretch cord
- ☐ jeweler's glue

To make a Stretchy Bracelet with Sliders:

- *If your slider string isn't quite long enough for a bracelet, thread on a few coordinating beads to extend the length.*
- *If your sliders have 3 sets of holes or loops on the back, use three 12" cord lengths in Step 1.*

1. With bead stops *(Fig. 1)* at the ends of two 12" cord lengths, thread the sliders and seed beads (if using) on the cords.
2. Check the bracelet size, adding or removing sliders or beads until the bracelet is the right length. Tie the cords with surgeon's knots *(Fig. 2)* and apply a drop of glue to each knot. Once dry, trim the ends. Add a ribbon bow, if desired.

Fig. 1

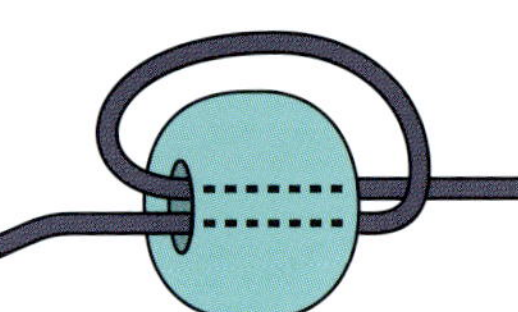

Fig. 2

To make a Stretchy Bracelet with Beads:

- *If your bead string isn't quite long enough for a bracelet, thread on a few coordinating beads to extend the length.*

1. With a bead stop *(Fig. 1)* at the end of a 12" cord length, thread the beads and optional charm on the cord.

2. Check the bracelet size, adding or removing beads until the bracelet is the right length. Tie the cord with a surgeon's knot *(Fig. 2)* and apply a drop of glue to the knot. Once dry, trim the ends.

1 String, 7 Necklaces

SHOPPING LIST

- ☐ flat colored stones string
- ☐ 4mm and 6mm silver beads
- ☐ braiding cords that match the stones
- ☐ silver foldover cord ends
- ☐ silver lobster clasps
- ☐ silver jump rings
- ☐ jeweler's glue
- ☐ chain-nose pliers (2 pair)

To make each Necklace:

Approx. Length: varies

1. Cut the desired length of braiding cord. Thread silver beads and a large stone on the cord. You can let the silver beads loosely fall next to the stone or tie knots to hold the silver beads in place further away from the stone.

2. Lay one end of the cord in the foldover cord end, apply a drop of glue, and use the chain-nose pliers to fold the tabs down over the end of the cord *(Fig. 1)*. Repeat with the opposite end of the cord.

Fig. 1

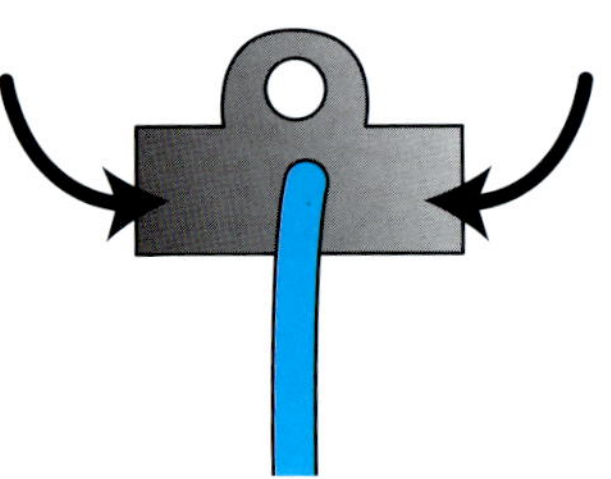

3. Use a jump ring (page 31) to attach a clasp to one cord end.

How many times have you seen these colorful, abstract stones and wondered "How can I use those?" Well, just get some matching color braiding cord to make seven different necklaces–one each for you and six friends.

Big Stone Rings

SHOPPING LIST

- ☐ large stone bead
- ☐ assorted coordinating beads
- ☐ 22-gauge wire
- ☐ adjustable ring with flat pad
- ☐ jeweler's glue
- ☐ wire cutters and chain-nose pliers

To make each Ring:

1. Slide the large stone bead on a 24" wire length. Thread the wire around the ring pad; use the chain-nose pliers to wrap the wire around the stone and the ring to hold the stone in place. Add a bit of glue to hold the stone on the ring pad.

2. Thread the assorted beads on the wire ends. Twist and wrap the wire and beads around the large stone and ring as desired. Twist the ends to secure, trim the excess wire, and hide the ends.

Have a single stone? Make a rockin' ring! Crissed-crossed wire and smaller beads pull it all together.

GENERAL INSTRUCTIONS

TOOLS

Chain-nose pliers have rounded, tapered jaws and a flat interior surface that will not mar wire. These pliers are used for reaching into tight places, gripping objects, opening and closing jump rings, and bending wire.

Round-nose pliers have round jaws that are useful for making loops and bending wire smoothly.

Wire cutters are used to cut small gauge wire, head pins, and eye pins.

A crimp tool (also known as crimping pliers) flattens and shapes the crimp bead or crimp tube.

TECHNIQUES

Opening and Closing Jump Rings, Chain Links, or Loops on Eye Pins/ Head Pins

Pick up a jump ring with chain-nose pliers. With a second pair of chain-nose pliers, gently hold the other side of the ring. Open the ring by pulling one pair of pliers toward you while pushing the other away *(Fig. 1)*.

Fig. 1

Close the ring by pushing and pulling the pliers in opposite directions, bringing the ring ends back together. Open and close chain links and loops on eye pins or head pins the same way.

Making a Bead Dangle, a Connector, or a Loop on Wire

A bead dangle is made on a head pin and has a loop at the top. Connectors are made on eye pins and have loops on both ends. Loops on wire ends are made in the same manner as the loops on bead dangles and connectors.

Slide the beads on a head pin or eye pin. Leaving about $^1/_2$", cut off the excess wire. Using chain-nose pliers, bend the wire at a 90° angle *(Fig. 2)*. Grasp the wire end with the round-nose pliers. Turn the pliers and bend the wire into a loop *(Figs. 3-4)*. Release the pliers. Straighten or twist the loop further if necessary.

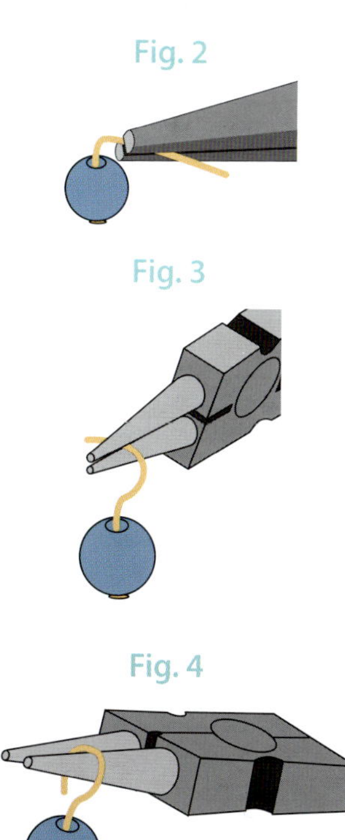

Fig. 2

Fig. 3

Fig. 4

Using Crimp Beads

To finish a wire end, thread a crimp bead and the clasp or jump ring on the wire. Run the wire back through the crimp bead; use a pair of pliers to pull and tighten the wire *(Fig. 5)*. Place the crimp bead on the inner groove of the crimp tool and squeeze *(Fig. 6)*.

Fig. 5

Fig. 6

Release the tool, turn the crimp bead a quarter turn, and place it in the outer groove *(Fig. 7)*. Squeeze the tool to round out the crimp bead *(Fig. 8)*. Thread beads over the wire to cover the short end.

Fig. 7

Fig.8

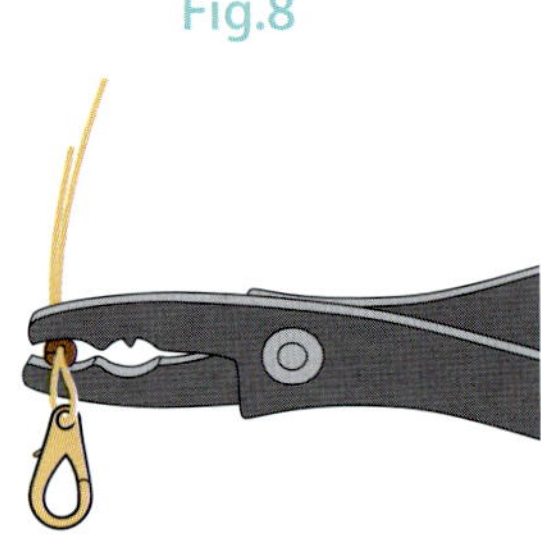

Tying an Overhand Knot

Hold the cords together and tie an overhand knot *(Fig. 9)* near one end.

Fig. 9

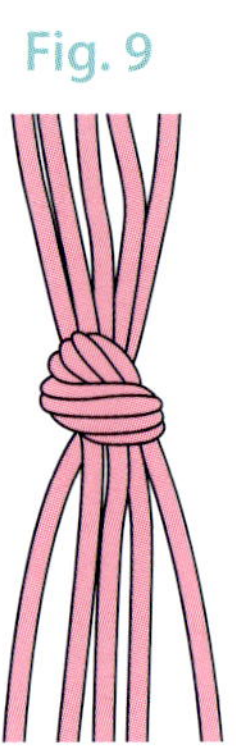

Tying a Square Knot

Use the outer cords to tie the first half of a square knot around the center cord *(Fig. 10)*. Tie the second half of a square knot *(Fig. 11)*.

Fig. 10 Fig. 11

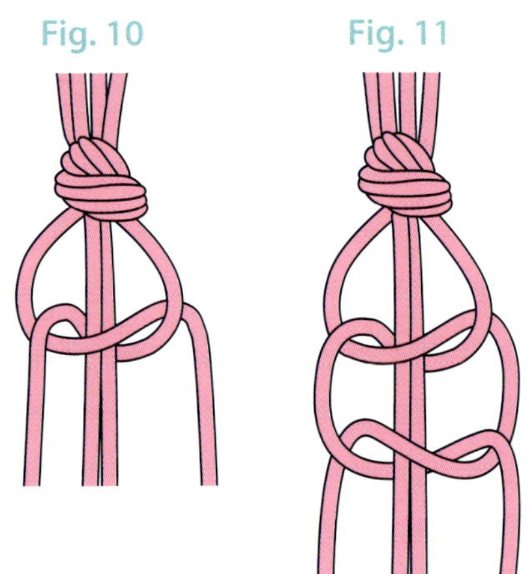

Production Team: Crafts Design Director – Patti Wallenfang; Designer – Kelly Reider; Technical Writer – Mary Sullivan Hutcheson; Technical Associate – Jean Lewis; Editorial Writer – Susan Frantz Wiles; Senior Graphic Artist – Lora Puls; Graphic Artist – Cailen Cochran; Photostylists – Sondra Daniel and Lori Wenger; Photographers – Jason Masters and Ken West.